Holy Island

Text by M. Scott Weightman, BA
Photographs by Caroline Claughton, ARPS

Published by
Claughton Photography
PUBLICATIONS

First published in this form 2000
Originally published by M. Scott Weightman

History

St. Oswald King of Northumbria
St. Aidan and St. Cuthbert

In 634, Oswald, a Christian convert, following years of exile in Scotland, defeated Cadwallon, King of North Wales, and reunited the Kingdoms of Bernicia and Deira. From his capital at Bebbanburgh (Bamburgh) Oswald established Northumbrian supremacy from the Humber to the Forth. It was Oswald who sent to Iona for a missionary. Corman, the first missionary, found the Northumbrians 'uncivilised people of obstinate and barbarous temperament' and he returned to Scotland. Soon after, in 635, Aidan arrived in Northumbria.

Aidan chose Lindisfarne, close to the royal residence at Bamburgh, and secure in its island position, as the site for his church and monastery. From this base, Aidan preached the gospel throughout Northumbria, King Oswald sometimes acting as his interpreter. The mission flourished, lands were gifted for ecclesiastical purposes, churches and monasteries were founded and children were sent to be educated by the Scottish monks. Four of the children who arrived at the monastery school were brothers, Cedd, Cynebil, Caelin and Chad. All four

St. Cuthbert's Isle can be reached at low tide. Bede says that Cuthbert used a small chapel here. Today the site of its altar is marked by a wooden cross.

boys eventually became priests and two, Cedd and Chad, were ordained as bishops. Chad was sent to Ireland by Aidan and, having completed his studies, he returned to Northumbria, where he worked as a bishop. It is recorded that Chad was a gentle and devout man, similar to Aidan in his devotion to his work. He was venerated as a saint after his death in 672 and pilgrims visited his tomb in the belief that it held powers of healing.

The presence of Aidan's mission on Lindisfarne changed the Northumbrian people. According to Bede 'many Northumbrians, both noble and simple, laid aside their weapons, preferring to take monastic vows rather than study the art of war'. Missionaries trained by Aidan travelled throughout Britain, some even journeying to the Netherlands. During his lifetime, communities of nuns were founded in Northumbria and Hild, the first Northumbrian woman to take the veil, was appointed Abbess of Hartlepool. The See which Aidan had founded was to last for almost 250 years.

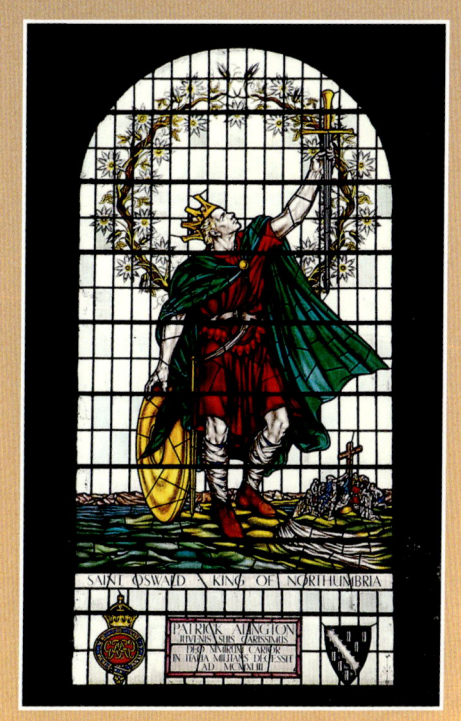

A window in Durham Cathedral by Hugh Easton showing St. Oswald, King of Northumbria, armed with his sword as his cross, and haloed by a garland of flowers.

The sixth bishop to succeed was Cuthbert (685-687), previously a shepherd on the Lammermuir hills. As a young man he was attached to the monastery at Melrose, the first and most famous of the 'cells' established by Aidan. He served briefly as Guest Master at the new monastery at Ripon, subsequently returning to Melrose Abbey as Prior. In 676 Cuthbert followed Aidan's example and sought seclusion on the Inner Farne. He remained on the island for nine years, living in a cell and oratory designed to isolate him from anything, even views of the land and sea, which may have distracted him from his prayers and meditation. It is said that during this time Cuthbert through the strength of his prayer performed miracles, many of which are recorded by the Venerable Bede. He was eventually persuaded by King Ecfrith, a nephew of Oswald, and Theodore of Tarsus, Archbishop of Canterbury, to become Bishop of Lindisfarne. He was consecrated at York on Easter Day, 26th March 685 and spent two years striving to bring a new unity to the Church in Northumbria. In 687 Cuthbert returned

A statue of St. Aidan, who founded the first monastery on the island. A Celtic cross frames the head of St. Aidan, who holds a torch symbolizing the light of the Gospel in one hand and his Bishop's crozier in the other.

to the solitude of his cell on Inner Farne, eventually dying on the island. His body was brought back to Lindisfarne and buried, with great honour, on the south side of the altar in the priory. Eleven years after his death the body was disinterred and it was reported by Bede to be uncorrupt. 'It was lying on its right side wholly entire and flexible in its joints, and resembling rather a person asleep than one dead.'

For more than a century after Cuthbert's death the See of Lindisfarne flourished, becoming more affluent and influential as the Church grew in England. However, the country was disorganised politically and was vulnerable, through the lack of an established armed force to repel any invaders. The Vikings, sailing from the United Kingdom of Norway, Sweden and Denmark, found the rivers convenient access routes to the interior of the country, where the treasures of the churches and monasteries provided rich plunder. On 7th June 793, the invaders reached Lindisfarne, burning the settlement and killing many of the monks. Symeon of Durham records, 'They came like stinging hornets, like ravening wolves, they made raids on all sides, slaying not only cattle but priests and monks. They came to the church at Lindisfarne, and laid all waste, trampled the Holy places with polluted feet, dug down the altars and bore away the treasure of the church. Some of the brethren they slew, some they carried away captive, some they drove out naked after mocking and vexing them. Some they drowned in the sea.' The survivors rebuilt the church but Northumbria gradually lost its power and influence and in 875 the monks fled from the monastery for fear of further invasion. In their terror, they took with them their precious holy relics, the body of St. Cuthbert, the skull of King Oswald, some of St. Aidan's bones and the Lindisfarne Gospels. It is probable that the laymen who had lived on the island also deserted the settlement and followed the monks to the mainland.

The body of St. Cuthbert was protected by the monks during the subsequent years. Seeking constantly to avoid the threat of invading Vikings they went first to Chester-le-Street, then fled to Ripon in 996 for fear of a Danish invasion. The body was returned to Durham but in 1069 was carried back to Lindisfarne when William the Conqueror seemed poised to subdue the rebellious North of England. In 1070, St. Cuthbert's body was taken back to Durham and has rested there ever since. The coffin was opened in 1104 and again in 1537 when the body was reported to be 'sound, sweet, odoriferous and flexible', 840 years after his death. Between 1542 and 1827 the grave was again disturbed and the body removed to a secret place allegedly known to only three people, and their successors, in a determined attempt to keep the saint's remains safe. There is a strong tradition that the body was moved to another part of Durham Cathedral and that it is there to this day. It is certain that St. Cuthbert's ring was taken from his finger and is used by the Bishop of Newcastle each time he ordains a priest.

The Pilgrims Way, marked by posts across the sands for the benefit of pilgrims, strangers and islanders.

Lindisfarne Gospels

A decorated page at the beginning of St. Luke's Gospel.

The Lindisfarne Gospels are one of the finest surviving examples of Celtic art. They were written in honour of St. Cuthbert by Eadfrid (Bishop of Lindisfarne 698-721). The use of the Greek word for saint, *Agies*, instead of the Latin, *Sanctus*, is significant and occurs throughout the Gospels where the Evangelists are named. The rest of the Gospels are written in Latin.

The Gospels were among the holy relics taken by the monks, who fled from Lindisfarne in 875. Legend states that the book was lost at sea and subsequently miraculously recovered during an attempt to remove the body of St. Cuthbert to the safety of Ireland. In the twelfth century, the Gospels were in Durham, but their history after this date is uncertain. It is unlikely that the rich adornment of jewels and gold was left untouched during the dissolution of the monasteries but there is no record of what happened to the Gospels until the seventeenth century, when it was noted that they were in the hands of the Clerk of Parliaments. Sir Robert Cottin subsquently acquired the book and the Gospels now lie in the British Museum.

St. Matthew with a winged man blowing a trumpet.

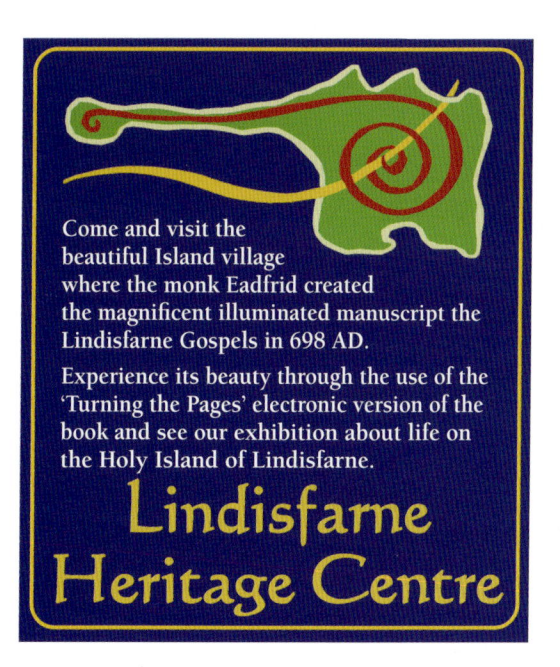

Come and visit the beautiful Island village where the monk Eadfrid created the magnificent illuminated manuscript the Lindisfarne Gospels in 698 AD.

Experience its beauty through the use of the 'Turning the Pages' electronic version of the book and see our exhibition about life on the Holy Island of Lindisfarne.

Lindisfarne Heritage Centre

Lindisfarne Priory and the Parish Church of St. Mary

Following the monks' departure from Lindisfarne in 875 it seems probable that the island remained uninhabited for more than two centuries. In 1082 a cell of Benedictine monks was granted the See of Lindisfarne and renamed the island 'Holy Island' to commemorate the holy blood shed during the invasions of the Vikings. Since that time, there has always been a settlement on the island. The monks rebuilt the ruined priory, dedicating it to St. Cuthbert on its completion in 1120. Sandstone was the material chiefly used, some quarried on the island but most brought from Goswick on the mainland. The present ruins of the building are an impressive testimony to its past elegance and stature. There was no significant alteration to the priory until the fifteenth century, when the apse at the east end of the chancel was demolished, the chancel lengthened and made oblong in shape.

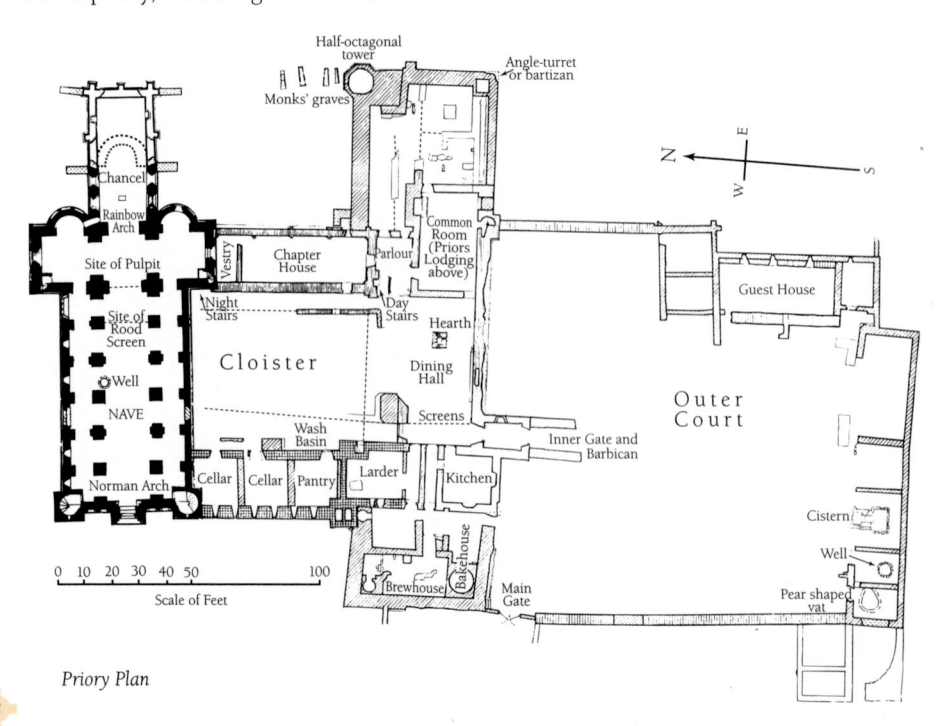

Priory Plan

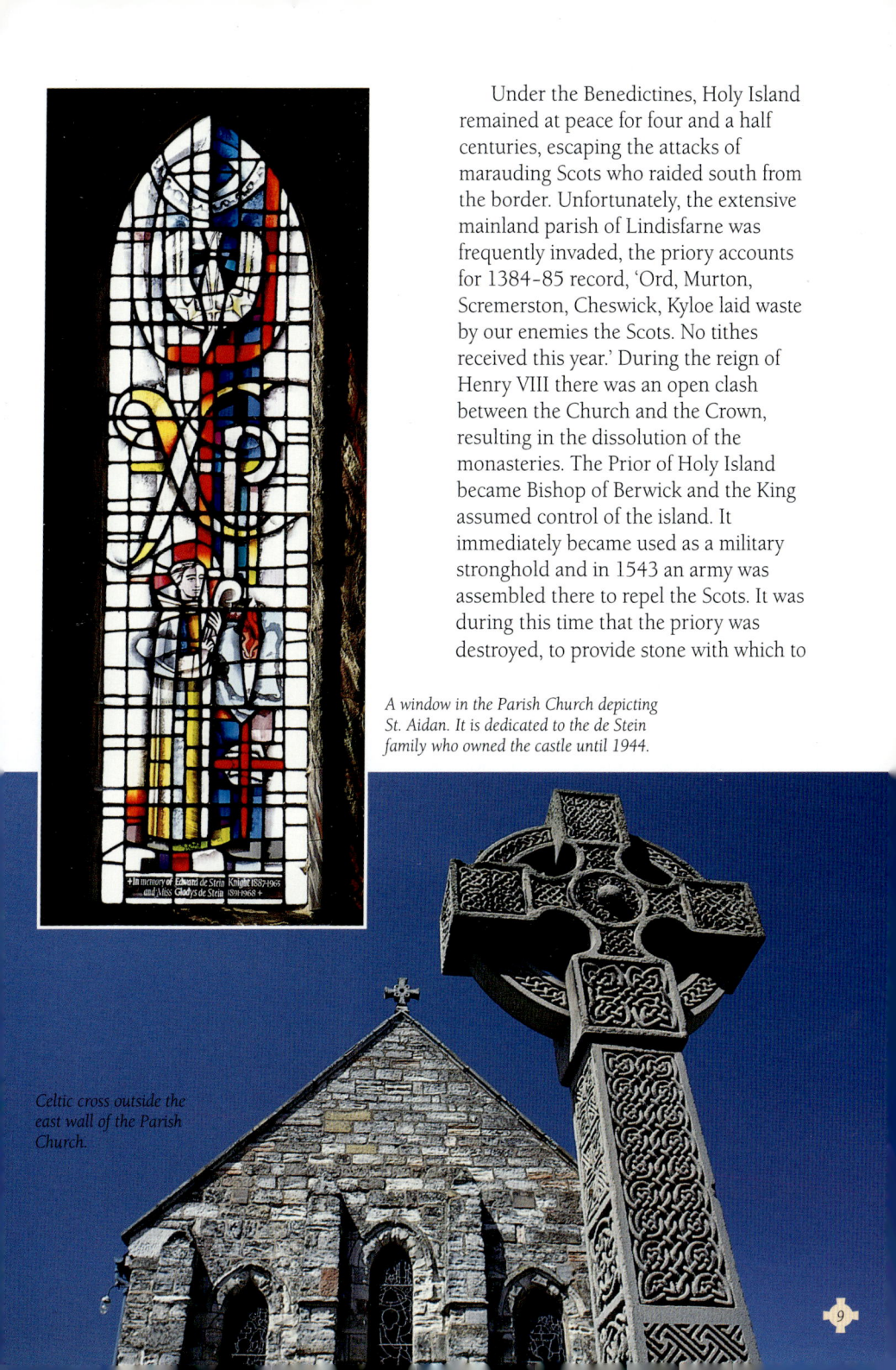

Under the Benedictines, Holy Island remained at peace for four and a half centuries, escaping the attacks of marauding Scots who raided south from the border. Unfortunately, the extensive mainland parish of Lindisfarne was frequently invaded, the priory accounts for 1384-85 record, 'Ord, Murton, Scremerston, Cheswick, Kyloe laid waste by our enemies the Scots. No tithes received this year.' During the reign of Henry VIII there was an open clash between the Church and the Crown, resulting in the dissolution of the monasteries. The Prior of Holy Island became Bishop of Berwick and the King assumed control of the island. It immediately became used as a military stronghold and in 1543 an army was assembled there to repel the Scots. It was during this time that the priory was destroyed, to provide stone with which to

A window in the Parish Church depicting St. Aidan. It is dedicated to the de Stein family who owned the castle until 1944.

Celtic cross outside the east wall of the Parish Church.

build the new castle. The priory church was converted into a store house 'for the King's use'. In 1550 the cell of the Benedictine monks was referred to as 'the Queenes Majesties store house' and in 1613 Lord Walsen, Earl of Dunbar, ransacked what remained of the priory, removing the lead from the roof, the bells and anything else he considered of value. The ship carrying the stolen materials sank shortly after leaving the island and many of those aboard were drowned, an act said to be indicative of God's displeasure at this further desecration of Holy Island.

The roofless ruin of the Norman church is the most spectacular feature of what remains of the priory. The west front contains the main entrance, used only on ceremonial occasions when the monks would process through into the church. The doorway has an impressive rounded head, decorated with a zigzag design. The wrought iron gateway was a much later addition, donated to the church in 1840 by the then Lord of the Manor. Above the entrance is an open gallery of five arches and on either side are pillars, the remains of what was a Norman arcade. The church was cruciform in shape and over the centre of the cross is a magnificent vaulting rib, the Rainbow Arch. This architectural detail and the ornamental design on the arch and pillars in the church, suggest that it was built by the same monks who built Durham Cathedral, where similar patterns were used. The monks' living quarters were clustered around a cloister on the south side of the church. On the left of the south transept are the remains of a small spiral staircase, the night stairs used by the monks to go to church services straight from their dormitory. Although the design of the monastery is Benedictine the community of monks on Lindisfarne was a small one and so the buildings were adapted to suit their needs. They were also fortified as a measure against the Scots, the entrance to the cloister from the court on the south side has a gate strengthened by a barbican. To the east of the cloister was the chapter house, on the west were the domestic areas, kitchen, brewhouse, pantry, cellars, larder and a bakehouse and on the south side was the dining hall. The priory guest house was in an outer court on the south of the monastery.

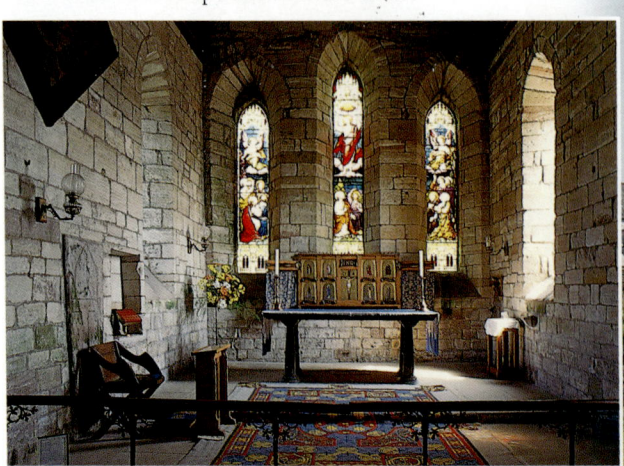

The chancel of St. Mary's, showing the carpet which reproduces a page from the Lindisfarne Gospels.

The Parish Church of St. Mary was built between 1120 and 1145, the original Norman architecture remaining in the form of three arches on the eastern side of the north aisle. The chancel is thirteenth century and there is a medieval tombstone, decorated with a cross and sword, on the north wall. There was a small belfry added to the church at the beginning of the eighteenth century and the major restoration was completed in 1860. There are two porches in the church; until 1886 the north porch was used as a mortuary for bodies recovered from the sea, it is now a vestry. The beautiful carpet before the altar was designed to reproduce a page of the Lindisfarne Gospels and the work was directed by Miss Kathleen Parbury. Students from Alnwick College of Education transferred the design on to the canvas and eighteen women from the island completed the needlework. The carpet was dedicated in June 1970. The Lindisfarne Gospels are also represented by a copy of the works given to the people of Holy Island by the Rockford College Community, Rockford, Illinois in 1970.

The eleventh-century entrance through the west front of the church is unmistakably of Norman design.

Lindisfarne Priory was built to re-establish a Christian community on Holy Island following the evacuation of the island after Viking raids in 875 AD.

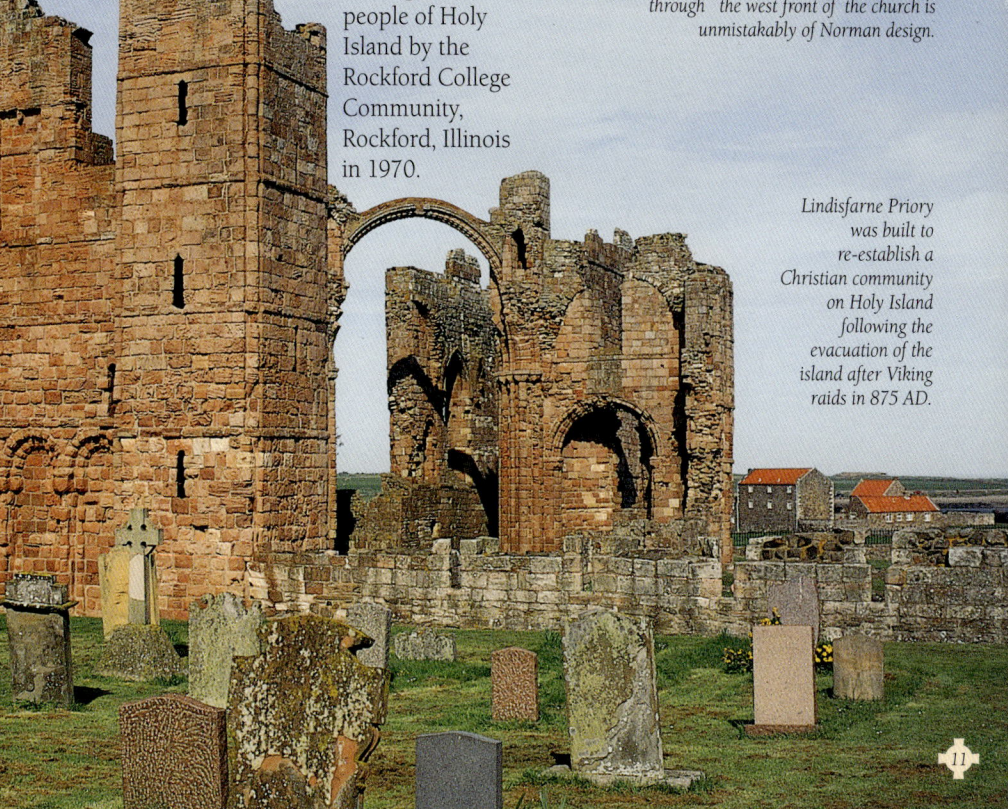

Lindisfarne Castle

The atmospheric beauty of Lindisfarne castle and harbour at dawn.

The first mention of the castle or fort appears in a Border Survey of 1550, carried out by Sir Robert Bowes and Sir Ralph Ellerker in which they write of the 'Fort of Beblowe' (the ancient name of the hill on which the castle is built). The building began during the reign of Henry VIII, using the stone from the priory. Robert Rooke of Berwick superintended the first fortifications, which followed an order in council that 'all havens should be fensed with bulwarkes and bloke houses against the Scots'. In 1543 the castle had been the focus of a large army led by Edward Seymour, Earl of Hertford, (brother to Henry VIII's Queen, Jane Seymour) with the intention of fighting the Scots. The expedition was formed on Holy Island with the troops garrisoned there and ten line-of-battle ships at anchor in the harbour. Following the union of England and Scotland the strategic importance of the castle diminished, although it remained in use as a garrison. Troops were still stationed in the castle in 1639, when an officer of the King visited the island and reported on the good maintenance of the fort and its armaments, and the fact that a force of twenty-four soldiers and a captain were in post.

At the beginning of the Civil War, the castle was a Royalist stronghold but soon fell to the Parliamentarians. The next recorded incident was in 1715 when, having been reduced to a garrison of only seven men, five of whom were absent at the time, the castle was captured by two Jacobites. Unfortunately the reinforcements they expected failed to arrive and the two men eventually surrendered to a force of soldiers sent from Berwick to retake the stronghold.

In 1820, the guns were removed from the castle and it was partially dismantled, its use as a fortification being ended. Having been converted to a coastguard station, in the 1880s the castle was bought by Edward Hudson, the proprietor of *Country Life* and restored for him as a private residence by Sir Edward Lutyens. In 1944, the then owners, Sir Edward de Stein and his sister, gave the castle to the National Trust. A commemorative stained glass window in memory of Edward de Stein and Gladys de Stein can be seen in the Parish Church of St. Mary.

The castle, now owned by the National Trust, is perched on the highest point of the island, Beblowe Crag, an outcrop of dolerite in the sandstone.

Natural History

Lindisfarne has long been famous for its wildlife. The habitats of sand, mudflat, sand dunes, and saltmarsh provide much of interest for the birdwatcher, wildfowler, botanist and others with more general interests in natural history and the out of doors.

The saltmarshes and the botanically rich calcareous dune 'slacks' (low lying areas ringed by sand dunes) hold the most important plant communities on the island. Both of these habitat types are becoming increasingly rare in the north-east and are consequentially of high conservation value.

Much of the saltmarsh on the Reserve is dominated by Cord Grass (*Spartina*), a species which is obvious as soon as one drives on to the causeway from the mainland. However, on the south side of the island, a more diverse marsh community is found, with species such as Sea Aster, Scurvy and Sea Marra Grasses, and Thrift very much in evidence.

The sand dunes are covered chiefly by Marram Grass, the principal dune forming plant which, through the accretion of wind

Puffins are often observed fishing around the island.

The eider duck is the best known and most numerous of our sea ducks. According to legend, St. Cuthbert loved the eider duck above all other birds and it is locally known as St. Cuthbert's or Cuddy's duck.

blown sand, both builds up and stabilizes the dune. Houndstongue and Viper's Bugloss are conspicuous flowering plants on the more stable dunes while the 'slacks', mentioned previously, support a rich flora crowned by the Meadow and Northern Marsh Orchids. The earlier stages in the plant and dune succession of an exposed sandy beach are seen along the north-east shore of the Snook in the form of Sea Couch and Sea Lyme Grasses.

Lindisfarne is famous chiefly for its overwintering wildfowl and waders, where it is of considerable national and international importance.

Wigeon, the most common duck species and major prey for the wildfowler, with a peak count of 25,962 present in the 1982-83 winter, placed Lindisfarne first in importance for this species amongst British and Irish estuaries. In the same winter the flock of 1,800 pale bellied Brent belonging to the Spitsbergen breeding population was the only gathering of any size recorded in England, Scotland or Wales. The overwintering numbers of Whooper Swan peaked at 96 at the same time making the area one of the most important for Whoopers in England. These three species feed primarily on Eelgrass, the beds of which are found from the high to the mid-tidal zone.

Other species of geese, swan and duck which are usually seen are Greylag Geese, Mute Swan, Mallard, Teal and the occasional Pintail.

Off the coast, Eiders, the Common and frequently the Velvet Scoter, often four species of grebes and the Great Northern and Red-throated Diver, are present, particularly during the winter months. Two of the best locations to observe the sea-ducks, grebes and divers are from Ross Back Sands and Emmanuel Head. From the same locations and during the summer months various other sea-birds such as Gannets, Puffins and Guillemots are often observed.

Thrift is very much in evidence in the diverse marsh community of plants.

Of the waders overwintering at Lindisfarne, Dunlin, Knot, and Bar-tailed Godwit are the most numerous but Curlew, Redshank, Oystercatcher and, to a lesser extent, Grey and Ringed Plover are also fairly abundant. The less common Turnstone and Purple Sandpiper are found frequenting the more rocky coastal area of the Reserve. During migration, Sanderling and Whimbrel are generally present but the bird-watcher may also observe Greenshank, Spotted Redshank and Little Stint. The waders feed on the great numbers of shellfish, worms and crustaceans which inhabit the mud and sandflats. In winter, quite spectacular flocks of waders are to be seen flighting north over the causeway and Snook to their high water roosting areas as the flood tide approaches the causeway. Several wader species breed at Lindisfarne among which are Ringed Plover, Oystercatcher and Redshank.

Little and Sandwich Terns are the two most prominent members of this family breeding at Lindisfarne. The number of nesting Little Terns has decreased lately, and the public should take especial care not to disturb them.

The birds of prey comprise another group of particular interest. Short-eared Owls and Kestrels are resident throughout the year and the Merlin and Sparrow Hawk are regularly seen during the winter months, often chasing smaller waders.

Lindisfarne is of great interest for the ornitholigist during spring and autumn migration when, under favourable wind conditions, the unusual as well as the more common migrants may be sighted. Warblers, thrushes and finches, for example, pass through the area in great numbers. Many of the more common British song birds breed in the sand dunes, hedgerows and gardens of the island.

With such a variety of species present during the seasons Lindisfarne indeed deserves its prominent place in the view of the bird-watchers.

The most notable geological feature is undoubtedly the dolerite dyke to the south of the island. This forms some of the most spectacular relief, particularly at Lindisfarne Castle, a natural fortress, where the dolerite intrusion is about sixty-five yards wide. The dyke disappears in the Ouse, perhaps a result of faulting, but it reappears in the ridge to the south of the village. St. Cuthbert's Island is also formed of dolerite.

Fulmars nest on the top of the old limekilns. If an intruder approaches too near, the fulmar spits a pungent stomach fluid rich in vitamin A at the danger.

Island Community and Links with the mainland

The route across the Holy Island Sands to Chare Ends, used in the time of Saints Aidan and Cuthbert, remains the only access to the mainland. Tides sweep across the sands with great speed and have caught many people unawares - the parish register records several deaths as the waters caught unwary travellers. The crossing remained virtually unchanged until the beginning of the twentieth century, the only improvement having been the positioning of posts to mark the route in 1860. Pilgrims, strangers and islanders were all dependent upon these markers to guide them across the sands. Most people walked from the mainland to the island, the photograph below shows two island fishwives who took their donkeys to carry fish for sale in Berwick and Belford. The other main form of transport, the horse and cart, was

Island fisherwomen 1857. In the past, fisherwomen took fish to the mainland to sell, loading their donkeys for the trip.

of restricted use on the island, very few islanders being able to own a pony cart. The owners of two public houses, the Crown and Anchor and the Northumberland Arms, and the postmaster, all enjoyed this luxury and allowed their carts to be hired out. There was also a carriage and pair which frequently made the journey to Berwick but the most popular 'transport' link with the mainland was the post cart, with a regular two journeys each day. At high tide when the sands were flooded, boats were used. The only other way of contacting the mainland, the telephone, was installed in 1920, with one line available for islanders to use. This service has now been extended to cope with the increased demand on the island, a new exchange being opened in 1974.

With the advent of the motor car the pony and traps were replaced by taxis, although the post continued to be carried by pony trap until 1954. The vehicles used as taxis were especially adapted to cope with the journey across the sands, their engine and car bodies being raised to avoid the danger of water damaging the cars.

In 1954 the causeway was opened and formed a permanent man-made link between Lindisfarne and the mainland, thus creating the end of the island as a separate unit.

The Pilgrims Way marks the most direct route from the mainland to Chare Ends. The refuge boxes are provided for the safety of unwary travellers.

Holy Island's causeway was opened in 1954. Tide tables are provided along the route to remind travellers of the dangers.

In 1965 the road was extended and the part crossing the channel of the South Low was elevated above the level of the sands. This improved access has encouraged more people to visit the island and enabled all vehicles to drive from the mainland, thus removing the need for the characteristic 'Holy Island' taxis. The link with the mainland was reinforced in 1972 when the United Bus Company set up a regular bus service between Berwick and Holy Island. However the island community still retains its independence and separate identity from the mainland, a quality enforced by the sea, which still floods the causeway and renders the link with the mainland impassable for two hours before and three and a half hours after each high tide. (The tidal flow still traps unsuspecting visitors and the refuge box, built to provide an escape from the encroaching water, is still in use, particularly in the summer months.)

Farming and fishing were the first economic activities on the island. The monks who initially settled on Lindisfarne organised the agriculture of the parish as well as the island and tithes were drawn from Beal, Fenwick and Fenham. The land was extremely profitable and the only problem encountered came from the Scots, who regularly plundered the crops as they invaded south. The efficiency of this farming system was destroyed when the monasteries were dissolved in 1537. A report to the Crown in 1561 recorded the poverty on the island and noted that most of those living there were fishermen.

Limekilns at Castle Point. The quarrying of limestone was recorded back to 1344, and in 1860 the Dundee Company built a new landing-jetty below the castle.

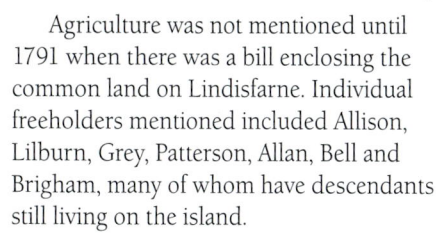

Upturned herring boats are now used for storage.

Agriculture was not mentioned until 1791 when there was a bill enclosing the common land on Lindisfarne. Individual freeholders mentioned included Allison, Lilburn, Grey, Patterson, Allan, Bell and Brigham, many of whom have descendants still living on the island.

The island people have an obvious involvement with the sea and fishing is also a traditional occupation. The first record of the trade is in the priors accounts of 1372 when sums of money were noted to pay for building boats and buying herring nets. The fishing trade increased throughout the years and by the nineteenth century had developed into a prosperous occupation, catches included crab, cod, lobster and herring and two-thirds of the island's population were engaged in cleaning and catching the fish. In the 1860s there was a large fleet of thirty-six boats but, as Eyemouth and Seahouses became increasingly important as mainland fishing ports, the Holy Island fleet declined and by 1875 only twelve boats remained. By the beginning of the twentieth century the island had ceased to be regarded as a significant fishing centre and now only a few boats sail from here mainly seeking catches of shellfish. The upturned herring boats are a reminder of the once flourishing industry and the old smoking sheds used to prepare the fish are still in evidence, converted into dwellings.

Where the growing herring fleet once anchored in the Ouse estuary now the pleasure craft of visitors and residents are moored. However, the original fishing boats were also used to salvage booty from ships wrecked in nearby waters and there was some suspicion voiced in the seventeenth century that the islanders were deliberately luring cargo ships on to

It is thought that Snook Tower housed winding-gear for an eighteenth-century coal mine.

the rocks in order to steal their loads. These suspicions may well have been founded on fact but whatever damage was caused by earlier inhabitants on Holy Island, the establishment of a lifeboat station provided adequate recompense. The first lifeboat was launched in 1829 and a second boat was subsequently stationed at Snook Point. In 1875 the *Grace Darling* lifeboat rescued thirty-five survivors from the steamer *Britannia*, of Leith and in 1904 the Admiralty awarded £1,000 to the lifeboat crew who rescued the *Harcola*, a vessel of 5,000 tons, in particularly dangerous seas. In 1907 there were still two lifeboats on Holy Island, an inshore boat and a heavier vessel used in the open sea around the Farne Islands. The last boat to be stationed on Lindisfarne was withdrawn by the R.N.L.I. in 1968.

Mining was also an established occupation on the island, from the time the monks built the original priory using local sandstone. In the fourteenth century the quarrying of limestone was recorded and there was still quarrying and burning of limestone five centuries later at the Snook and the Coves. In 1860 the Dundee Company built the kilns below the castle and although the lime industry ceased towards the end of the nineteenth century, the kilns and the embankment, along which the horse drawn wagons drew the stone, are still well preserved.

Iron ore has also been mined, in the seventeenth century the Carron Iron Company carried iron ore to its furnaces on the Firth of Forth. Coal was dug on the island, the tower at the Snook is the shaft of the small mine worked there. The seams were only six inches thick and were worked for only short periods, an attempt to revive the industry in 1840 failed after two years and there has been no further interest in the mine except during the General Strike of 1926, when the villagers sought to acquire their own supplies of coal.

The island today has lost much of the peace and tranquillity of past centuries. During the tourist season the island throngs with visitors. Only in winter does Holy Island assume its former character and once again have its individual air of a place, at peace apart from the rest of Britain.